IRAQ

By Sloane Gould and
Ruth Bjorklund

EXPLORING
WORLD
CULTURES

Cavendish
Square

Published in 2024 by Cavendish Square Publishing, LLC
2544 Clinton Street, Buffalo, NY 14224

Second Edition

Website: cavendishsq.com

Library of Congress Cataloging-in-Publication Data

Names: Gould, Sloane, author. | Bjorklund, Ruth, author.
Title: Iraq / Sloane Gould and Ruth Bjorklund.
Description: Second edition. | Buffalo, NY : Cavendish Square Publishing, [2024] | Series: Exploring world cultures | Includes index.
Identifiers: LCCN 2023011161 (print) | LCCN 2023011162 (ebook) | ISBN 9781502667496 (library binding) | ISBN 9781502667489 (paperback) | ISBN 9781502667502 (ebook)
Subjects: LCSH: Iraq--Juvenile literature.
Classification: LCC DS70.62 .G68 2024 (print) | LCC DS70.62 (ebook) | DDC 956.7--dc23/eng/20230308
LC record available at https://lccn.loc.gov/2023011161
LC ebook record available at https://lccn.loc.gov/2023011162

Writers: Ruth Bjorklund; Sloane Gould (second edition)
Editor: Caitie McAneney
Copyeditor: Shannon Harts
Designer: Andrea Davison-Bartolotta

The photographs in this book are used by permission and through the courtesy of: Cover ESB Professional/Shutterstock.com; p. 4 Peter Hermes Furian/Shutterstock.com; p. 5 Felix Friebe/Shutterstock.com; p. 6 Karrar A. AlAwadi/Shutterstock.com; p. 7 Darbaz Dara/Shutterstock.com; p. 8 Jukka Palm/Shutterstock.com; p. 9 HansFree/Shutterstock.com; p. 10 NVM Design/Shutterstock.com; p. 11 Angela N Perryman/Shutterstock.com; p. 13 (top) Zety Akhzar/Shutterstock.com; pp. 13 (bottom), 22, 29 Mohammed_Al_Ali/Shutterstock.com; p. 14 Ondrej Chvatal/Shutterstock.com; p. 15 Lena Ha/Shutterstock.com; p. 16 John Wreford/Shutterstock.com; p. 17 photoringo80/Shutterstock.com; p. 18 Sadik Gulec/Shutterstock.com; p. 19 thomas koch/Shutterstock.com; p. 21 (top) Muhannad Faour/Shutterstock.com; p. 21 (bottom) Red Stock/Shutterstock.com; p. 23 Billion Photos/Shutterstock.com; p. 24 stockce/Shutterstock.com; p. 25 kerenby/Shutterstock.com; p. 26 mooinblack/Shutterstock.com; p. 27 Marla_Sela/Shutterstock.com; p. 28 Maksim Denisenko/Shutterstock.com.

CPSIA compliance information: Batch #CS24CSQ: For further information contact Cavendish Square Publishing LLC at 1-877-980-4450.

Printed in the United States of America

CONTENTS

INTRODUCTION

Iraq is rich in history, land, and **culture**. Some of the oldest **civilizations** in the world called this land home. An ancient place called Mesopotamia was located where Iraq and Kuwait are today, between the Tigris and the Euphrates Rivers. Rich land allowed Sumerian, Assyrian, Akkadian, and Babylonian civilizations to grow.

Iraq shares borders with Iran, Jordan, Kuwait, Saudi Arabia, Syria, and Türkiye.

Today, many people call the region, or area, that includes Iraq the Middle East. The people who live in Iraq are called Iraqis. The country is home to many tribes, both small and large. In some areas, there is fighting and struggle, but there's also a rich **tradition** of music, food, and celebration.

The land in Iraq is very diverse, which means it has different parts. It's home to rocky deserts, mountains, and wetlands. Like ancient peoples, today's Iraqis mostly live in the fertile, or rich, plains by the Tigris and Euphrates. Let's explore this ancient and diverse country!

Akre is a city in northern Iraq's Kurdistan region.

GEOGRAPHY

If you look at a map of the world, you'll find Iraq in southwestern Asia. The Tigris and Euphrates Rivers are important to Iraqi people and animals. Flowing across Iraq, these rivers historically have rich floodplains that support farming. Farming today is harder due to **drought**, though. Fish, birds, and ducks make their homes along the rivers. Many animals, such as hyenas and foxes, live in the hills and plains.

Baghdad is Iraq's largest city. It's on the Tigris River.

Northeastern Iraq includes part of the mountain region of Kurdistan.

FACT!

Iraq is part of the Fertile Crescent, a region in Western Asia and North Africa where civilization began.

Iraq is almost completely surrounded by land, with just a small bit of coastline. In the northeast, there are mountains. At about 11,847 feet (3,611 meters) tall, Cheekha Dar is the highest mountain in Iraq. Southern Iraq has both rocky deserts and marshy land.

SEASONS

Iraq has two main seasons. In summer, it is dry and either warm or very hot. In winter, rain or snow fall in some places.

HISTORY

The Fertile Crescent is often known as the "cradle of civilization." Each civilization in today's Iraq created something new. The ancient Babylonian ruler Hammurabi (who ruled in the 1700s BCE) created one of the world's first sets of laws.

FACT!

Great Britain took control of Iraq after World War I (1914–1918).

These ruins are part of the ancient Babylonian palace of King Nebuchadnezzar II.

In the seventh century CE, Arabs gave Iraq its name. Iraq means "fertile" in Arabic. It became a world center for learning, culture, and trade. Later, civilizations like the Romans, Greeks, and Ottoman Turks ruled Iraq. Then, Great Britain took over. Iraq gained independence from Britain in 1932.

In the 1980s and 1990s, a **dictator** named Saddam Hussein led Iraq into many wars. In 2003, the United States captured Hussein. Iraqis dealt with the fighting and **terrorism** that followed, working to build a new government.

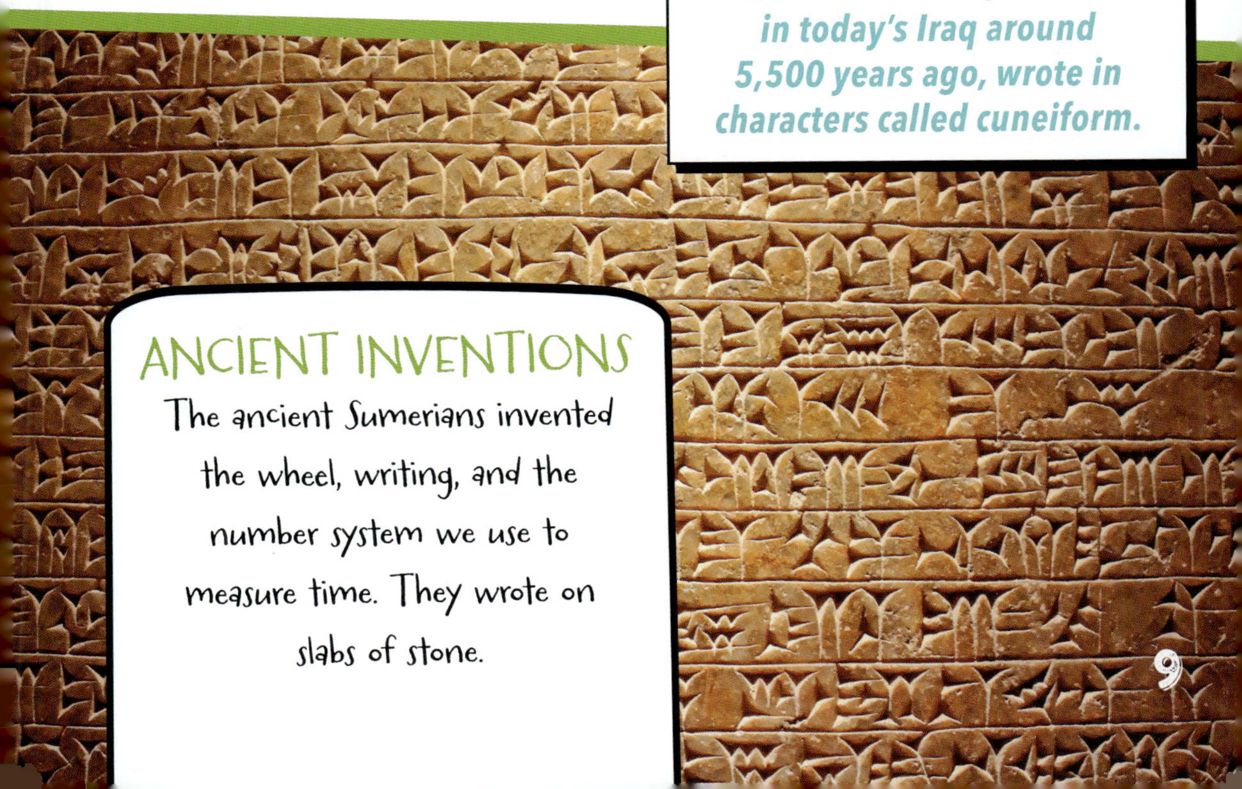

Ancient Sumerians, who lived in today's Iraq around 5,500 years ago, wrote in characters called cuneiform.

ANCIENT INVENTIONS

The ancient Sumerians invented the wheel, writing, and the number system we use to measure time. They wrote on slabs of stone.

GOVERNMENT

When Saddam Hussein was in power, he ruled harshly. He was very rich while many of his people were very poor. He ordered many crimes against **human rights**, including killing and jailing people. Two years after he was captured, lawmakers wrote Iraq's current **constitution**.

FACT!
The official name of Iraq is the Republic of Iraq.

Iraq's flag has three stripes. Black means war, red means bloody struggle, and white means goodness.

Iraq's government is divided into three branches: executive, legislative, and judicial. People vote for their leaders. The president heads the executive branch. There are up to three vice presidents and a prime minister.

The legislative branch, known as the Council of Representatives, makes laws. There are 329 members. The Supreme Court is one of the highest courts in the country.

GOVERNORATES

Iraq is split into 19 parts, called governorates. Each has a governor to lead it. The self-governing Kurdistan region is home to the Kurdish **ethnic** group.

Many parts of Iraq, including the capital of Baghdad, had to be rebuilt after war with the United States that began in 2003.

THE ECONOMY

For thousands of years, Iraq has been rich in **natural resources**. On farms, Iraqis grow wheat, rice, corn, dates, figs, grapes, and cotton. People also raise goats, sheep, and chickens. They sell milk, eggs, meat, leather, and wool.

In 1927, oil was discovered there. Most of Iraq's wealth comes from selling oil to other countries. Other natural resources in Iraq are salt, stone, and natural gas. Iraqi workers make cloth, leather, and metal products.

However, wars have hurt Iraq's economy—its system of buying and selling goods and services. For many years, the government didn't handle the economy well. However, Iraqis are hardworking. Some are teachers, bankers, and doctors. Others are construction workers, cooks, maids, taxi drivers, and oil workers.

FACT!

More than 99 percent of the money Iraq makes from selling goods and services to other countries is from oil.

Iraqi money is called the dinar.

OPEC

In 1960, the Organization of the Petroleum Exporting Countries (OPEC) was founded in Baghdad. OPEC makes decisions that affect oil prices and supply.

This farmer picks dates in Basra, Iraq.

THE ENVIRONMENT

Iraq has had a beautiful environment, or natural world, for much of its history. However, Iraq has many environmental problems today. Cars, trucks, and factories dirty the air in cities. Dirty water from houses, roads, and factories runs into rivers, lakes, and the sea. Droughts and sandstorms cause problems.

FACT!
Camels and gazelles are found in Iraq's deserts.

Persian leopards are endangered, or at risk of dying out, in Iraq.

Iraq has many oil wells and towers. Burning oil sends harmful gases into the air. This makes some Iraqi people sick.

When Saddam Hussein was in power, he bombed and drained the Mesopotamian Marshes. He wanted to punish, or harm for certain actions, the Marsh Arabs who lived there.

AN IMPORTANT HABITAT

Iraq has many fish, birds, reptiles, and mammals. Iraq's government is making laws to keep them safe.

Today, parts of the Mesopotamian Marshes have been restored. However, droughts harm the marshes.

THE PEOPLE TODAY

As of 2023, more than 40 million people live in Iraq. The main ethnic group in Iraq is Iraqi, or Mesopotamian, Arab. Arabs are people who speak Arabic and whose **ancestors** came from the Arabian **Peninsula** in southwestern Asia.

FACT!
Iraqi Arabs make up about 75 percent of Iraq's total population.

About 40,000 Marsh Arabs live in southern Iraq.

Iraqi Arab tribes are divided into smaller groups, called clans and *khams*. The khams is a family group based on all the male children who share the same great-great-grandfather.

About 17 percent of Iraqis are Kurdish. The Kurdish region has its own prime minister, flag, national song, and army. Turkmen and Assyrians are other Iraqi groups. Each group has their own language and ways of life. This makes the country diverse.

These Kurdish children in Iraq are **refugees**.

CITY LIVING

Most Iraqis live in cities such as Baghdad, Basra, and Mosul. Nearly everyone lives near the Euphrates and Tigris Rivers.

LIFESTYLE

Family is very important in Iraq. Each household may hold parents, children, grandparents, aunts, uncles, and cousins. As families grow, more rooms are added onto the family house.

Some families in Iraq are refugees from other countries who live in camps.

VALUES

Parents teach their children to be loyal to family, tribe, and country. Parents share their values about honor, education, and respecting elders.

Men work outside of the house. Women are usually expected to cook, clean, and raise the children. In recent years, more women have gotten an education or have worked outside the home. The average birth rate in Iraq is about 3.6 births per woman.

More boys than girls go to high school in Iraq. Many children in poor families stop going to school at a young age and have jobs. Years of war and moving for their safety have made it hard for some children to go to school.

FACT!

People walk, use cars, and take trains to get around Iraq.

Iraqis walk around Baghdad.

RELIGION

The official religion, or belief system, of Iraq is Islam, and most Iraqi people follow this religion. Iraqi laws follow the laws of Islam. People who follow Islam are called Muslims. There are two branches of Islam, Sunni and Shia.

Muslims follow the teachings of the Prophet Muhammad. Muhammad said Allah, his god, wanted him to preach Islam. Muslims follow the laws of Islam. They say that there is no other god but Allah. They also pray five times a day; give money to the poor; fast during the holy month of Ramadan; and make a journey to Mecca, Muhammad's birthplace in Saudi Arabia. These are called the Five Pillars of Islam.

FACT!

Most Muslims in Iraq are Shia.

OTHER RELIGIONS

Some Christians, Jews, and people of smaller native religions live in Iraq. However, they are not always treated well.

Mosques are holy buildings for Muslims.

Muslim women often cover their hair with a covering called a hijab.

LANGUAGE

Arabic is the most widely spoken language in Iraq. Nearly all Iraqis speak Arabic. Other languages are Kurdish, Turkmen, Farsi, Armenian, Syriac, and Persian. Kurdish is the second-most spoken language in Iraq. Arabic and Kurdish are Iraq's two official languages.

FACT!

More than 371 million people speak Arabic as a first language around the world.

People read Arabic right to left.

There are 28 letters in the Arabic alphabet. Arabic writing uses special marks, such as dots, over the letters. It's the language of the Quran, or the holy book of Islam. That makes Arabic an important language to Muslims all over the world.

Arabic storytellers have been writing stories and poems since ancient times. Some traditional folktales are still told and read today.

THE ORIGINS OF ARABIC

Arabic came from the Arabian Peninsula. The Quran helped spread Arabic around the world.

This is the Quran.

ARTS AND FESTIVALS

Art has been important in Iraq since ancient times. Ancient peoples of today's Iraq left behind paintings of battles and royalty. They also left pottery and jewelry. Artists of the past and present use gems and clay tiles to make patterns. These patterns are called mosaics. Mosaics decorate walls, pathways, and buildings.

An Islamic string instrument called the oud (pictured here) is often played in Iraq. It is the parent of the lute known in Europe.

For celebrations such as weddings and the New Year, Iraqis enjoy special foods, music, and dancing. For religious holidays, Iraqis pray together with family and friends. Eid al-Fitr is a three-day holiday at the end of the Muslim holy month of Ramadan. It's one of the most important celebrations of the year.

FACT!
Iraqi Independence Day is celebrated on October 3.

RAMADAN

During Ramadan, Muslims don't eat between sunrise and sunset. It ends with Eid al-Fitr, a time when Iraqis gather with friends and family, eat sweets, and give gifts.

Mosaics decorate many mosques and walls.

FUN AND PLAY

Iraqis have dealt with war and fighting for many years. However, they also have traditional games just for fun. Kids play soccer, also called football, in dusty fields and streets. Soccer is the most popular sport. The Iraqi national team has competed, or tried to win, in the World Cup and the Olympics.

FACT!

The National Iraqi soccer team is called the Lions of Mesopotamia.

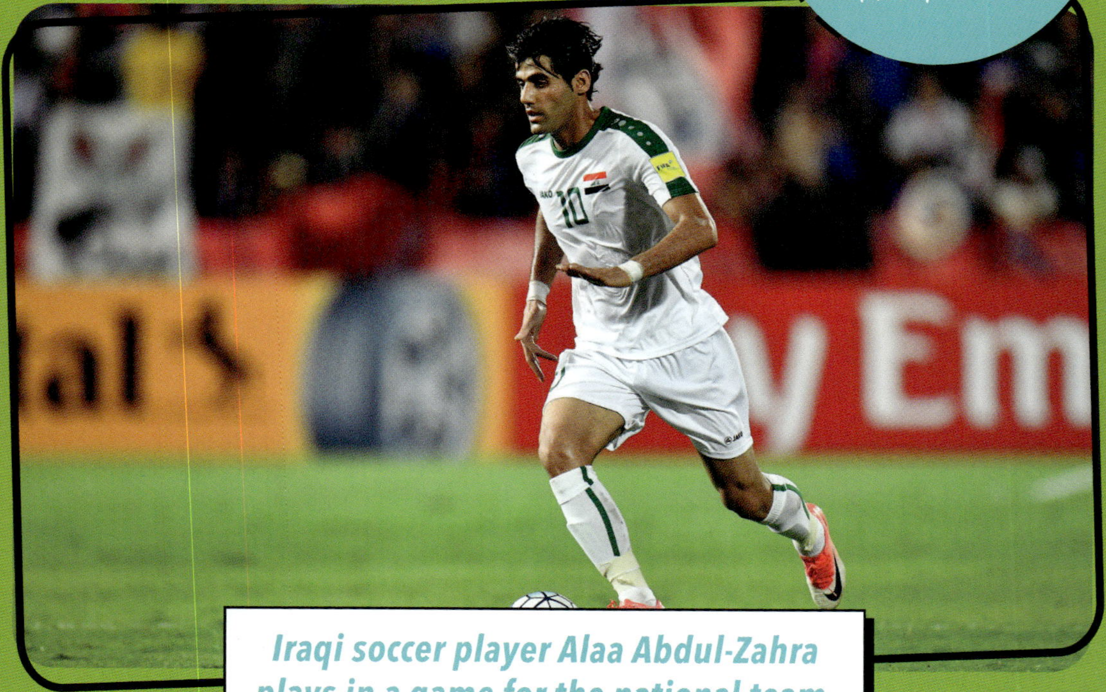

Iraqi soccer player Alaa Abdul-Zahra plays in a game for the national team.

It is not traditional for girls to play sports, but today, there are some girls' and women's basketball teams. As shown in the movie *Salaam Dunk*, playing sports was so new to Iraqi girls that many had to learn how to dribble before learning how to shoot a ball through a hoop.

Indoor games include chess and dice. In modern times, some Iraqi kids play video games too.

Kids play in snow in the Kurdistan region of Iraq.

MHEIBIS

During Ramadan, many play a game called mheibis in which teams hide rings from each other.

FOOD

Eating meals together is a big part of Iraqi life. Iraqi people cook with many fruits and vegetables, as well as meat such as lamb, beef, and chicken. Honey is a popular food. Iraqi people have been beekeepers for thousands of years!

Some of the most common foods in Iraq are kebabs and dolmas. Kebabs are grilled meat on a stick. Dolmas are grape leaves stuffed with spiced rice. Many combinations of meat and grains are eaten.

Eid al-Fitr, the end of Ramadan, is celebrated with huge feasts.

People in Iraq love to drink tea. Special foods include pastries, or desserts filled with nuts and spices. Iraqi food is just as rich as the other parts of its culture!

FACT!

Most Iraqis won't eat pork because it is against the laws of Islam.

Many meals are cooked outside over a fire.

RAMADAN FASTING

During the Ramadan fast, people wake before dawn to eat a meal. Then they don't eat all day. After sunset, they have iftar, a full meal often eaten in large groups.

GLOSSARY

ancestors: Family members from whom a person has descended.

civilization: An organized society with written records and laws.

constitution: A document that describes a country's laws.

culture: The beliefs and ways of life of a certain group of people.

dictator: A person who rules a country with total power and often in a harmful way.

drought: A long period of dry weather.

ethnic: Relating to large groups of people who have the same origin, religion, customs, and more.

human rights: Rights that all people in the world should have because they are human beings.

natural resource: Something that is found in nature and is valuable to humans.

peninsula: Land surrounded on three sides by water.

refugee: Someone who is seeking a safe place to live, especially during a time of war.

terrorism: The continuous use of violence and fear to challenge an authority.

tradition: A way of thinking, behaving, or doing something that's been used by people in a particular society for a long time.

FIND OUT MORE

Books

Andrews, Elizabeth. *The Mesopotamians*. Minneapolis, MN: Pop!, an imprint of ABDO, 2023.

Islam, Burhana. *Amazing Muslims Who Changed the World*. London, UK: Penguin Random House Children's UK, 2021.

Website

Iraq

kids.nationalgeographic.com/geography/countries/article/iraq

Explore Iraq's geography, nature, and history with *National Geographic Kids*.

Video

Mesopotamia

www.youtube.com/watch?v=QeZKNjo-exs

Learn more about ancient Mesopotamia!

Publisher's note to educators and parents: Our editors have carefully reviewed these websites to ensure that they are suitable for students. Many websites change frequently, however, and we cannot guarantee that a site's future contents will continue to meet our high standards of quality and educational value. Be advised that students should be closely supervised whenever they access the internet.

INDEX